73

Strange Light
poems and stories

 og

by Derrick C. Brown

Write Bloody Publishing
America's Independent Press

Long Beach, CA

WRITEBLOODY.COM

Brown, Derrick C.
1ˢᵗ edition.
ISBN: 978-1-935904-65-6

Interior Layout by Lea C. Deschenes
Cover Designed by Nik Ewing
Photos by Mike McGee
Proofread by Jennifer Roach
Edited by Tara Hardy, Courtney Olsen, Mindy Nettifee, Amber Tamblyn, Loulu Losorelli, and Adrian Wyatt

Type set in Bergamo from www.theleagueofmoveabletype.com

Special thanks to Lightning Bolt Donor, Weston Renoud

Printed in Tennessee, USA

Write Bloody Publishing
Long Beach, CA
Support Independent Presses
writebloody.com

To contact the author, send an email to writebloody@gmail.com

*for Paratroopers, Sailors, Motorcyclists
and people who kiss with their all on the first date.*

STRANGE LIGHT

(STRANGLE LIGHT)

STRANGE LIGHT

LOVERS FIZZ

Remind me of Spain.
Let the propane
light from the barbecue
glow the back of your hair into
silhouette.

Set.

Scuttle the plans,
drive with the radio off,
peel out in the gravel,
drive like a Trucker that's been punched,
put WD-40 on the box spring and feel sneaky,
stand in front of the mirror with a camera waiting
for the love of your life to show up.

Don't be Amsterdam, be Holland.
I've never been to Spain. I'm asking you to remind me of it.
Don't just be tits, be all the tits, be wanted.
Don't puss out on love.
Put some ice cream in the *dead man's float*.
You're either someone's dinner or you're someone's genius,
either way doesn't matter as long as you're zizzing delicious.
Allow me to be an ocean, allow me to freeze.
I'm saying I can hold you up,
even the waves retreat to make room for new ones.
I want to forget all endings that demand paradise.
Terror moves me.
Scream into a road map 'til the lungs are transmission hot:

Dear Lord, is that all you got?

Some giant in the sky pushes
the head of night down
into the sea
and a crown of stars bubbles
on up. Fizzle that way.

Ringlets

Young prom ladies in loud dresses and ringlets
    mingle outside the restaurant in oversized
        men's suit jackets, their dates, smile-smoking,

        shivering, pretending not to shiver. The thing
    you said was dead is not dead. No virgin deserves
a cigarette. We should head to the emergency room

and just pop our heads in and say hello. Tell them we
    are alright so they don't think we only visit when
        things are bad. We are breathing without tubes today.

        They don't make pills yet for this feeling. It's like finding
        fruit
in the snow. I want to call down cocktails and black tire
jacks from the heavens. I want to break into something.

That kind of good. Your eyes are the kind we have all been waiting for.
When I hear a single note sustain in a room
    with bad lighting, I think of us.

    Both of our bodies,
        shivering.

Our Long Low Nights

1.
Sometimes when a jazz cymbal
is played with a brush—
a steady soft roll—
I hear those rainy streets,
the cars I shoved you against,
kissing you into place.

I can hear *them* coming for us,
rolling across the wet asphalt.
Our shirts as skin, soaked tight.
We both hate poems that mention jazz,
which is okay, because jazz hates us.
We kiss like jazz hates us.

2.
You're not scared of living,
you're not scared of love,
you're not scared of money, sex or the truth,
but there's never enough.

3.
Walking at night, you said Life is a midget dog.
It might be short and bewildering
but remember: don't look down or back or open your hand,
and if it bites you, it is correct
to punch it straight in the neck.

4.
We're standing in the kitchen with no ornamentation,
two Christmas trees tired of religion. Tired of the dishes.

You're brilliant when you're exhausted.
We don't know what to do tonight.
Walk to the grocery store and play Find the Best Smell.
Buy a month's worth of paper plates.

5.
In the cupboard I find corn silk powder.
When I am bored, I sprinkle some out on the floor and Bing Crosby
   in my socks.
It makes me miss the skin on the insides of your legs.

6.
You found a sledgehammer in the garage.
Someone with a sledgehammer loves me.
I rejoiced like Berlin.

We invented a game called Find Two Things to Smash.
We played it every night. Whoever found the most *"I should've
   smashed that a long time ago"* thing,
doesn't have to clean up. You want me to write you a book of these sounds.

7.
The kind of love that matters is
walking into the China shop with a 2x4 and waiting for the nervous
   clerk to say, "…can I help you?"
Then saying, "No, but I can help you."

8.
When your chest is heavy and full of colorful medals from the day,
I'll have beers and bath waiting.
If we don't have a bath, I'll find our biggest bowl.

9.
A horsewhip snaps—the sound barrier is broken. Even the laws of
   nature, even us.

10.
The poetry class taught me to start strong, end strong.
I am supposed to write down the greatest thing about you,
that I could imagine about you.

We ordered pizza.
We told our friends we couldn't meet up.
There were cherries and bourbon sauce in the fridge.
You dragged our mattress into the living room.
Turned out all the lights.

Watched an actor try too hard.
The phone didn't ring.
The commercials were funny.
I ran my fingernails down your arm.
We forgot napkins.

Nothing was on.
Nothing is on.

A Breeze Returning

1.
Young boy watches his balloon blow away.
No other balloon will do. *What if it never
returns?* The boy is wrecked.

One day later,
the boy forgets the balloon.
Finds large kite.

Kite reels home to him when he is tired.
He naps on it
in the breezy grass and does not wonder about the balloon.

2.
Teen boy confuses loneliness with insomnia.
Falls in love and gets good sleep.
Looks tired in class.

The roller rinks are at a constant state
of couples skate. In the general direction.
One woman is skating backwards. He starts to practice.

3.
Low Man felt like
he had outgrown the beach. Toes now in sand, looks
up to see boy, strapped to kite,
line anchored to a stone, waiting
to be reeled in
or cut free.

THE BEST
OR MANIAC SOUL PLUMBER

Texas is Jacuzzi fat.

Texas is lost in you,
in the mosquito dark.

Thank you dead Texas,
for putting the claim on my love.

Secede from Texas.

Come back to me, dear.
Come back to deer meat.
Texas is too hot and wide to be hugged.

I can't afford to touch you when you are in Texas.

Is your Christmas card going to be the entire death penalty?
Are you going to wear jeans that make your vagina plural?
Are you going to take pride in suicide being an outdoor nap?
Are you going to learn to not apologize for Abilene,
for it being as needy as us?

Come back to me. We can move to the pale Northwest.
Portland can't stop crying.
Bend Oregon is pretty nice if you like Californians.

Here
is best.

STRANGE HOURS IN NEW YORK CITY

Debris.

And the night was
          and then she.

Atsomecrowdedhotel.

Warm wind through the balcony rails.

Knock.

          Pond of blonde. Canary
yes.

Shows up tight as a bud. Suffering white and prayerless.

To get under her skirt and drown
in the radiant medicine of now.

To withdraw fantastic
into these strange hours with her
is now.

We have nothing to talk about.

"You can see ground zero from here."

Ya? I've seen it.

Her eyes do not move from mine.
I kiss her down. I kiss her closed.

It is sincere
to me.

The car she drove broke down
and I waited as she shook Long Island free from her bumper,
and I
watched the news
tell me what was dangerous.

I boiled and boiled.

The door opened, there stood:
42 love letters unreturned, 8 dildos, 15 cocks, 2 vaginas,
5 motorcycle hip holds, 3 slap fights, 1 chase via baseball bat, 112
    cold beers alone,
0 roses from lovers and 0 arrangements.

                The balcony door breezed.

One spirit was snowing.

The other was shoveling the driveway.
Museum hands digging into me,
her legs all lifejacket.

Nude and frust. Our bodies burned like wedding gowns.

I'm trying
to make you feel
geraniums. A kind
of flower you can
eat.

             Car keys and unopened wine on the dresser.

Something red
pumping fast and steady
on a machine
in her purse.

WHEN NURSES COUGH

When I first heard the nurse cough
I thought that she
wasn't very good at her job.

The second thing I thought
was that I don't trust bartenders
who don't drink.

I HATE YOU

When asked if he could change one thing in the world,
his answer wasn't any lame diatribe about One Love,
Affordable Housing or World Peace,
it was,
"I would like to make bread softer."

Anis, I hate you.

When asked what his dream date would be like
he said, "I'd rather someone else go who deserves it more.
I hope it goes well, I'm cooking a bowl of toast."

I detest you, Anis.

How is it possible that your name is one letter away from "anus"
and no one ever makes fun of that?
Everybody likes you to your face, but behind your back…
they like you even more.
WTF?!

I have odium for you, Anis.
…which I know you know means intense dislike, scholarship man!

I know you can only wake up when you smell cookies.
I know that when you read that "Footprints" poem before you sleep,
you often wonder if there was only one set of footprints
because Jesus and you were actually hopping with one leg
in a burlap sack race to baby heaven.
I loathe you with all my heart, Anis.
I hate that you sound like the Snuggle fabric softener bear during lovemaking.
I hope you choke on a lego. Do the bubbleguts!
Bend over the anvil, Anis, and get stretched.
It's not that I super-hate you, it's that I hate that I can't make
magic wholeness like you can.
A -holeness.

See you on America's Most Wanted… as a victim.

LE MONDE DU SILENCE

In a solo sub, you,
the lustwanderling,
wait for signs of life.

You hold the sea in your breath
and move in the thick puck of darkness.

Arms outstretched, full of loving mechanics.
Adrift in the wet pause of no one.
All fucked up on wanting.
All hungry for surface light and cherry flavored zippers.

A life in the pitch. You dream:
—The one where you high dive into tar pits and open your eyes.
—The one where you are alone in every bed, no matter who else is there.
Sometimes knife.
—The one where more people love you the more you destroy.
And then one night, in the dream state, a voice:

"Derrique, Derrique..."

Who's there?

"It is Jacques Cousteau, your Captain. Don't salute."

How did you get in here?

*"You craftily left the key under the mat, fringe-head. You obviously want
someone to break in so you have someone to talk to or fight. Surprise, He's French!"*

You're the great undersea explorer, inventor of the aqua-lung,
famed French ocean scientist.

*"Great? Greatest... undersea explorer. I am not a scientist. I am, rather,
an impresario of scientists."*

I apologize, didn't mean to make it seem I was attacking you.

"A lot of people attack the sea, I make love to it."

That sounds exhausting.

"Don't be so literal. Have some fun.
Don't be a doorknob, be a door."

Do you have a torch? Then I can see you.

"No. But I am octopying your space. That is a bad joke.
Cheer up, you brick."

Why does it feel like I am sinking?

"From birth, man carries the weight of gravity on his shoulders. He is bolted
to earth. But man has only to sink beneath the surface and he is free."

Are you taking me beneath the surface?

We…as in both of us. I am also not using quotation marks anymore.
So what's the dish? What do we do about your problem, Derrique?

What do you mean?

Two words. You Wallow.

I Hello?

No, you boob urchin. Wallow. You wallow in your darkness. You cover yourself
in it like a sand shark, lazy in the mire of the ocean floor.
What is the good of this?

I can't fake happiness. Happiness and pure joy are for people
who can dance sober and babies with banana gas.

The darkness is quiet sure comfort. The darkness is Alone, is safe,
is what I know. I go on and I'm fine.

If we go on the way we have, the fault is our greed and if we are not willing
to change, we will disappear from the face of the globe, to be replaced
by the insect.

But I wasn't born for that. I wasn't born into that.
I am a sudden flash, a soft shaking and blindfolded logic.

*If we were logical, the future would be bleak, indeed. But we are more
than logical. We are the magic ghosts called human beings, and we have faith,
and we have hope, and we can work. You should write down your sorrow.
All of it. Fill the dead sea. Leave it behind. Don't wait for it to come
up floating.*

I was born to be alone, you French tart. I wear weariness well.
I want to be a secret.

*When one man, for whatever reason, has the opportunity to lead
an extraordinary life, he has no right to keep it to himself.*

*Derrique,
You are a line in a short poem. You will be predatory for the neck of love.
And then gone.*

*It is not that you must refrain from hiding in the black, but you make the darkness
meaningless without the other half. For the light, we must search. You must
explore what this consciousness is, hands out in front of you. Hands wide
in front of you. Now is good.*

Goodnight Captain. I promise to search for brighter waters. Even if
the answers have all dried out.

I will meet you... at the crossroads. So you won't be lonely...

...and I'm gonna miss everybody.

*That's the spirit. Bon voyage. Don't dive alone. Bring a torch.
Wave it around. Something will be drawn to it. Bon noir!*

---

*　　80% of these quotations are directly taken from Jacques Cousteau.

*　　2% of these quotations were taken from the hit group, Bone Thugs-N-
　　Harmony. One editor told me this piece didn't work because this doesn't sound
　　like anything JC would ever say.

GIRL ON THE DOCKS

There are no girls on the docks. No women live on boats alone. I have lived on a cheap sailboat for years and the girls, or women, who do show up are scorched, like Stevie Nicks now, and on their third marriage.

Most sailors are single fathers burying their lawn mowers and fancy houses in favor of pouring their savings into the bilge. These men could use the comfort of a woman, but many are over the work of it.

It is so cold at night on the 30-foot long Billy Ocean; the white fiberglass walls are wet and feel like dry ice. I warm my sleeping cap in a pan over the propane stove and place it on my head. This boat is beating me up but the rent is right. All photos are warped. All clothing smells a little like fuel.

I can tell I've been here too long the same way I can tell when my razors have gone bad. Every night is dinner alone with the great silent passenger, its face glowing under me.

No girls live on the docks and I'm starting to see why.

I washed the chili-coated spoon in the sink while still in bed but couldn't finish the dinner cereal. I was going to throw the steel spoon away but I often don't want to get out from the covers 'til sunrise.

I have taken to not tasting food; just trying to swallow whatever is in the cupboard so my stomach doesn't bitch. I like eating food more than gussying it up. I can bite into a tomato and just get through it. This ship has taught me the ease and speed of small spaces. It has also taught me that I am not rich enough to care properly for any boat. I want meat. The fish are not biting. The flaking wood needs varnish. The weather makes me careless.

There is an old bottle of vodka I'm afraid to touch because it was left here by a girl named Mercedes. I don't think we screwed. If we did, I passed out during. She did not look like a Mercedes.

I look at the night reflection in the water and I remember houses coated in Christmas lights. I want those Christmas lights to fill up my hollow shaking legs. I close my eyes under the blue covers and remember, as a little boy, wanting to live among the Pirates of the Caribbean ride at Disneyland.

Tonight was my night to try force dreaming my boyhood vision. It worked. I was at the park in the ride. When you get in your boat with all the tourists, you'll see the big ships lobbing fake cannonballs — that's my spot, I wade out to it and rest by the second turret in the distance. Everyone is passing me by.

You can hear my modern voice say, "Beware the pigs, laughing. Beware the skeleton drinking wine. He never runs out. Beware the men chasing the women in the burning city. They never grow tired of the chase."

I wake up and peek out the teak hatch. I see long brown hair in the slip across from me, a backpack, young woman legs. Not a lot of gear with her. Quiet and respectful at night for the other sleepers. Sailors know to be this way. She lights a lamp. Tomorrow I will devise ways to make her wonder about me.

I hope she isn't named after something expensive.

The Gary Auction
of Spring Hill, Tennessee

Coke in a bottle is best
via machine. The concerned barker's call stopped
when it stole my money and the nacho lady had to help me.

One six-foot sickle.
One friar tuck tea pot.
One lamp of a bear, stealing
honey from a red tree.
Six pieces of dirty owl jewelry.
A pew built for one.
A small box of turquoise.
A working radio,
big as a desk.
A sewing machine from 1906.
A display case full of survival knives.
An oil lamp that burns slow.
A pendant of an onyx heart.
A case with a four leaf clover,
the glass cracked.

"We ain't selling no mattresses today, so ya all need to stop
sleeping. Start bidding."
The barker held up a few classic dolls:
"I'm not sure what material this is. I'm also not sure how all these
babies were made…well, I have some idea."
Paintings of slain ducks and rabbits, hanging by their feet:
I couldn't afford.
"Get your number."
The back barn is full of pianos.
Park in the grass, walk in and touch them all.
I bought the sickle.
When I went up to grab it:
"You know how to use that thing son?"
I told him, "I'm *dying* to learn."

The pulled pork and ice cream ain't the best,
but they're there.
Records.
Stuff the dead couldn't take.
No one to inherit it to.
If it was inherited, they called Gary
to get them some money.
Dust and tin.
The battle memorabilia.
Where will it go?
I learned what the old women loved: glass,
lamps, costume jewelry, intricate doilies, display plates of JFK,
and handmade blankets.
Everyone wants the confederate gear.

Stray Lightning

The feeling inside,
when you know there's fireworks,
but you're head's so heavy
you can't look up.

I know this hair is a dead willow mess,
this hair is Ally Sheedy in a staged blizzard and
these pants can pretend that celibacy is boring.
I'm often shirtless. I embarrass nature.

I know a vegetarian who eats horseradish
and doesn't think that's funny.

I don't get offended easy, I don't get easy enough.
I know the hard life of being a writer can leave you severely
dramatized.

I know why lightning is as jagged as us.
I know math is death.
I blow my money on magic no one else may see.
I stand at the back of punk shows, and church, and poetry readings,
waiting for someone to make me bouquet.

I know now I wasted much of my young life
putting up a wooden fence
around the volcano.

I know why people compare their lovers to ballrooms.
I need a suit.
I'll write my own invitation.

INSTEAD OF KILLING YOURSELF

wait until
a year from now
where you say,
"Holy fuck,
I can't believe I was going to kill myself before I etcetera'd...
before I went skinny dipping in Tennessee,
made my own IPA,
tried out for a game show,
rode a camel drunk,
skydived alone,
learned to waltz with clumsy old people,
photographed electric jellyfish,
built a sailboat from trash,
taught someone how to read,
etc. etc. etc."

The red washing
down the bathtub
can't change the color of the sea
at all.

No Walls, No Go

After the soft coals of sleep
the scratching at my bedroom door returns
and the noise
clings to the head like pools of blackstrap molasses,
raff-raff-straff- through my swampy pillows.

I used to see boars out my window.
Now the old, familiar Wolf-Fox of Sorrow,
Brimstone sifting through his smoking teeth,
blood in paws, low crawl in the grass,
he has come.

To crawl back inside me and weave himself in.
To chew out my insides and sew himself in.
The terrible sewing.

I woke up yesterday morning and
wanted to blow my brains out,
with a shotgun.
Two shells to blow my brains on the most beautiful wall—
the cleanest wall — a pool of milk waiting at the base—
the starkest white: eggshell or matte.

Spinning while exploding.
The mad spin. Walls catching me. Pink pink pink.
This so you can see what the Wolf-Fox has done
to me, has become to me.

I am fine with being the last of my name.

When I awake in our bed, hungry for these exit songs,
there is dust splitting the light.
There is that gaudy sky, all roofs on the ground,
and there are no walls for miles.

There is only rubble, settling dust, and a breeze.

You are standing there above me
with sledgehammer...exhausted.

Exhausted. Your shirt, a creek of sweat.
Your chest shining like a Colt Peacemaker.

Your voice is cashmere and rescue.

You say,
"My dear, true love is labor.
I will not learn how to love the dead.
No walls, no go.

There is nowhere to hang a calendar.
There is nowhere for clocks.

My love is for the living."

THE COMPANY MACHINE

SHE: Why won't you come to church with us? I have a bible for you. They're going to be talking about heaven and miracles.

YOU: Can we just imagine at some point in my life I realize that I have dirty clothes.

Everyone comes to a point where they realize they have dirty clothes, mine finally comes, the smell has finally gotten to me and only when I start to smell it can I decide to get my clothes clean.

If you call the company for me, I don't get to enroll in the benefits of their membership program. So time passes, and I am tired of the smell, so I call The Company. The Company tells me I can get rid of the smell, but I must get my clothes washed in The Company's washing machine.

I order it. It shows up and it is not assembled. It is wonky and confusing.

Much of it seems to have been designed at a time when we thought stars were lamps and the world was flat and you had to kill something to say you were sorry.

I am confused and instructed over the phone to go to a local company office to have a man in a strange suit show me how to disassemble it and then reassemble it so that the washing machine works correctly for me. Each company store interprets the manual differently. I chose the company office with the sauciest looking employees. They were cool, but they kept telling me to just feel it in my heart and I'll have it running in no time.

I decide to read the accompanying instruction manual to figure it all out for myself.

Some passages in the instructions are beautifully written and some are parables on how to assemble the washing machine.

I just want to get my clothes clean!
Why not say, just do *this* and you will see *this*!

The first half of the manual tells me how the boss is angry and jealous and the second half of the manual says how the boss of the company sends a piece of himself, the nice and poverty people loving side of himself, to teach everyone how to assemble these washing machines. He mentions that his employees make mistakes. He also mentions that his employees wrote the manual that he tried to dictate.

I try all day but I can't put this machine together with poetry. I decide that I do want clean clothes and I will wash them in the sink from now on, my way. So, thank you, but no I don't want to learn about heaven or resurrection from anyone as confused as me. Confusion bleeds through conviction.

SHE: Does everything in this life have to be so black and white?

YOU: Yes and no.

THE NIGHT: I come back all the time.

THE MEEK

Let the world hypnotize
me. The grocery store doors hushing.
The winding barbershop pole dervish.
The buttery lines in the road,
hyphenating black.

Frozen
and unfrozen. I am

a fast season. I get old and when I want it to stop,
music makes my mouth close.

Specter.

These puzzles
on the table don't need
to be finished.

Tomorrow is today to me,
a ghost with mail under his arm.

Vocoder Mango

I call you on your hotline. I ask what you're wearing.

You purr:
Twelve ounces of creamer in this skin,
Six gallons of God-carbon,
a necklace of eight balls and hair washed in a caramel bog.
Lipgloss made of yes bruises,
a gray and yellow ocean,
and one basket of wet black cherries.

You ask me what I'm wearing,
and I say:
"...something I thought the girl at the counter would like."

I ask you to sing for me the lonely sound.
You burst into clarinet,
you are instrument carved from a pipe bomb.
You sing:
I'm a woodpile. I'm the wood popping in the burning woodpile.
You know me, or you knew me. You fuel me, get warm from me
or get burns. Won't you come closer to the woodpile?

I know this song.
I love this song.

I ask you what you're really wearing,
and you say:
You sweet motherfucker,
I'm not even here.

PARTY DARKLY SPEED DATE

She is too sweet for my hands.
I keep them under the table.
I smell like meat.
She begins. *Nice place. I've never done this before.*
Me neither. I'll never do it again.

I'm Alpha November. So let's get down to it, what shapes you?
Divorce, hard work, the womb and death. Movies where everything blows up.
When were you divorced?
I've never been married. I have blown up.
I was a blockbuster summer. Now I'm the other thing.
The less people adore me, the more I am in control.

*Hi. I'm Foxtrot Lima. You do poetry. I can't tell when someone
is being poetic. Has poetry ruined you?*
Yes. The way tropical literature ruined you.

Hi, I'm Tango Echo. What's your favorite food?
Canned steak, Medium rare. And the juice. I like to get the juice on
    me.

Hi, I'm Bravo Charlie. I like sushi.
The smelly kind?
I like all sushi.
No you don't.
Yes I do.
Well I like all people.
Even the ones you haven't met?
See?
You're a grade-A ass.
You know that means the best ass.

Hi, I'm Hotel India. Favorite music?
Lonely and unashamed of lonely.

I'm Yankee Quebec. Would you like to visit a salt factory with me someday?
No. I just shaved.

*I'm Oscar Mike. Have you ever had the fear that you were asleep
and the house was full o flames?*
No. Oleanders.

I'm Golf. Have you ever taken a lovers survival getaway?
No. I don't like to mix the two. Or three.

I'm Zebra. Are you always an ass? And you don't care if you die this way?
I'm just nervous.

Don't Take Butter to the Beach

In 1943 Roosevelt and Churchill met
in Casablanca on January 14
to plot the strategies of freedom.

Casablanca as a film, Bogart's first romantic role,
freeing him from the limits
of being endlessly cast as a gangster.

His first character,
torn by love and virtue,
made him forever.

You are my
kind of
hokey Casablanca.

They will always say that
Citizen Kane is a better movie
but Casablanca is more loved.

I know you were born on January 14.

I know you plot the Wild Animal Park fence crashing
with your Honda,
the Double Decker bus rental,
with the sunroof for the zoo giraffe escape,
the Sea World penguin kidnapping
and whale homecoming blowhole party.
The restaurant lobster tank
liberation movement.

All these strategies for freedom
you plotted
for others. Now, you.

How did New York City get your number?
How dare it ring you after midnight
on a Tuesday.

There are too many people to love
in New York City.
You have to love them all or none. Do you have to go?

Call home. Call out for home. Call home something else.
Don't let them make you fast, possessed in satire.
Don't be Burroughs.
Be Lorca. Be Wakoski. Be Berrigan.

You're moving
is true in all ways.

You are from the un-photographed parts
of the Atlantic—
all that is hidden in you. Keep it.
I know it is ready to surface
into the black crotch of God light,
I hope the darkness tastes too sweet for you.

Your love is beach butter. Cover it up.
You don't have to bring it every time.

We cannot live
waiting
for the next heaven.

The clarinet was invented in Germany, 1690, on January 14.
Can you still sing out of your elbows? No?
Then you must sing with feeling.

January 14, 1956,
Little Richard released "Tutti Frutti".
Be careful where you release your Tutti Frutti.
You can run out.

I know.

January 14, 1976,
The Bionic Woman TV show made its debut.
Run faster than all things that are city sleek.
Do not close off.

Arms spread for maximum air acceptance.
Grow into your bionics humbly. Tell no one.

Wear my clothes.

Walk your shadow when the sun is setting.
Let it off the leash.

You can't out run it, anyway.

UNACCEPTANCE SPEECH

I would like to thank your automatic ass-fountain,
your adequate Iowa cornhole dumplumps.
Your frisky whiskey and laser colored piss test,
your figgy pudding-god-botched lip mess,
your inability to stop a beach cruiser after four drinks,
that made awareness of my own born-again-virginity possible.

You and me
are the same.

We both fight sexyism everyday.
You taught me that a woman's life is a human life.
'Tis better to drive a Suffragette than a Corvette.

You taught me that it is bad to sneak into a woman's house at night
to ask them if they know what a beef smoker is.

You turned this feminine mistake into *The Feminine Mystique*.

You used the phrase tijuana coin purse in a poem
when talking about your boob.
Gracias Senora.

You taught me to yodel during love making, on accident.
Yodelehehoo? Yo da lay he you!

I wanna kill your bikini,
DISCRIMINATE, DISCRIMI-NINE.

We've never owned Birkenstocks,
but we both loved Ani when she was gay.

Our favorite type of color, the color of manatee,
the hue-manatee.

CRYOGENICS IS NOT THE STUDY OF TEARS

The brochure in the lobby said in a bold, modern font...

The future is now, later.

And then in a smaller, wonky font:

You can relax knowing that the limits of time, aging and calendar dates are outdated.

KSCP treatment is the new and "relatively safe"* way to step into the bright light of tomorrow, today. By stalling the aging process through the use of modern cryogenics, KSCP can you help achieve your dreams.

What was that asterisk supposed to mean after the words relatively safe?

The back of the brochure had large stock photography with everyone looking like teeth-brightened models, like they never suffered a day in their soft, oversexed lives.

Play golf with your adult children.
Experience bizarre fashion and advancements in technology.
Outlive your friends.
Start a new life without having to bear children. New life is yours.
Cryogenics is the investment of a lifetime. The future is better.
You can sleep on it.

*FORMAL RISKS AND UNMEASURED PRECAUTIONS
TO CONSIDER FOR YOURSELF AND WHEN
CONSULTING LOVED ONES WHEN CHOOSING
THE KYMIA SYSTEMS CRYOGENIC PRESERVATION
TREATMENT:*

POSSIBLE SYMPTOMS

1.   *Loss of feeling in your extremities*
2.   *Memory loss in your extremities*
3.   *Loss of feeling in your memories*
4.   *A constant nippiness in the blood*

5. *Rickets and overwhelmitude*
6. *An immeasurable mistrust for the state of Alaska*
    and Christmas movies
7. *Longness of breath*
8. *Solid urine*
9. *A disconnect with the ones for whom you claim love*
10. *A lust for solitude when you are alone*
11. *Technological spite and forced living in Florida paranoia*
12. *Rosiness of cheeks and eager nutcracking*
13. *A sudden Tucson in the lungs*
14. *Stools shaped like stools*
15. *Chronic inability to distinguish Sweden from Norway*
    Often coupled with ignorance of Luxembourg
16. *White food guilt and dream deference*
17. *Loneliness confused with old timeyness*
18. *Inability to stay in love with someone smarter than you*
19. *Silence of the limbs*
20. *A constant appetite for what once was*

I told the Cryogenicist, Dr. Buck, a white haired mountain looking man in his sixties that some of these symptoms concerned me greatly.

"Which ones? Which symptoms?"

"Memory loss would be the thing I wanted to avoid the most. I like my memories. Even the bad ones. Even the hard ones. I can't imagine starting life at 35 years old, like a lost child, disoriented in the future. Trying to learn English and how to control my bladder. I need my memories... more than anything. If you could guarantee me safe passage through this program with my memories in tact, then I will sign."

He spoke of low percentages.

I asked him what it would be like, while I was under and frozen. I wanted details.

He said, *"You will enter a cold state but you will not experience the sensations while approaching the cold state. There will be no feelings of hypothermia as reported in some media outlets. We anesthetize the patients with a gas that works slowly and sends the patient into a dream state. Your body is kept alive and is reduced to -196 Celsius, but it still operates, just at an extremely slow state."*

"Can I wake up and freeze to death? Has that happened?"

He turned to the chart on the counter. *"In theory it could but it hasn't ever happened. We use liquefied gasses to bring your heartbeat to a reduced crawl. You are fed once a month through a tube. You get a small amount of nutrients to keep the dream sequence in continuity. You will wake up on the date stated in your contract. You will be dangerously dehydrated and we will keep you as an inpatient for 2 weeks to monitor your cell damage. You have enrolled in our 20-year program. May I ask why?"*

I fumbled with the glossy brochure. "Personal." He looked at me as if I owed him an answer. "I am waiting for someone."

"It is my job to give you safe and moral care during your stay with us, if I'm here when you come out. If not, someone new will be here in my place, which I know is a strange concept, but nothing you or I should fear. Now I'd like to have you recognize a few things you may not be thinking about. Many of your friends may be dead when you awake. You may hate the foods of the future. You may hate the way young people treat you, even though you'll look fairly young, your language, intellect and mannerisms could give you away. Can you be ready?"

I put my hands in my pockets. "I know I sound apprehensive, but I'm pretty desperate Doc. I can't sleep. I can't do anything. I'm a mess inside. Even if this kills me or blows all my savings, I need this."

Doc put his hand on my shoulder and nodded. I trusted him.

He twisted his blank white beard. *"We have had 2 patients perform our clinical trials of only 5 years. One did have significant memory loss. This patient preferred it due to some unfortunate events and addictions in his life. We tried a few procedures to keep his dream stasis a little darker. It did not erase his language or motor skills. I could arrange a call for you if you'd like to speak with him. Don't feel rude. He talks to people all the time in your shoes."*

I called the patient, Gary, the next evening. I had a few glasses of wine. I felt a little chicken about calling him. Gary spoke very deliberately and had the voice of a man who had lived in the south for eight to ten years. He told me personally of the waking status event he experienced.

Gary said:

"I wanted all them fuckers gone. Every last drop of memory. Every spool of hate and loss, kaput. So…. they definitely cranked something up on me, my choice. It was as if I was drifting upwards, reaching from a deep black pool of water, but I could feel like I was breathing more air than I could ever fit in my lungs before. I saw a pool. The pool was covered, and light was coming through the pool cover. My fingertips were kinda pushing through the elastic towards this, I dunno…warmth? Maybe it was sunshine. I could touch the light. I recall clearly that my bones felt like wet feathers, like they was cold from the inside, all packed with snow. I could feel my blood moving out from my heart to my fingers. Then it felt like it wanted out of my body. It was weird when it started to leave, right out my fingernails, towards the light. Streaming, just streaming like ribbons and droplets. It felt sooo good. I woke up, and then I didn't feel so good."

"Were you dehydrated?"

"I guess so," Gary took a long deep bite of some food. I could hear him chomping something crunchy in the receiver.

"What were you trying to erase?"

"I don't know. Ha. Haheha. I don't know. Effective as fuck. I looked at my shoelaces a few weeks later like it was got-damned trigonometry. I have no got-damned idea why I have this shitty accent either. Took me about a year to regain myself and not feel nutso. So, all I'm saying is it works if you want it to work. I recommend it. If ya got the bread." Crunch.

I thought about it for two days. All the What If's didn't frighten me. I went to the clinic in the steep-steep hills.

I began the paperwork and Doc came out from the waiting room door, looking like the Wizard of Oz wizard guy with his glasses perched on his nose.

"Legally I must remind you, there are risks of brittle bones, internal bruising, muscle atrophy, slight brain damage and all the other things mentioned in the brochure. Your eyes look ready."

I was. Even if it broke my body and warped my brain.

I walked down the hallway and hugged Doc. He spoke gently.

"I know she's worth it."

I couldn't tell if he said *was* or *is*.

Hours later, clothes off, they slid my table under a large rounded metal cover. The gas came to my mouth and had a slight lemon smell.

The deeper I went into sleep, the stronger and brighter my memories came to me. Then they began slipping away, in reverse…

I am riding a bicycle backwards through the park as the breeze pulls off of my body.
I am hiking to get to the bottom of a mountain.
I am sucking my name back into the pen from a late rent check.
Tears are sucking back up my face, into my dark sockets.

There is Arianna. Arianna.
I am watching a brown Buick reassemble in the night, ambulances appear in reverse, the front fender and hood is unbending back to normal. Arianna hurls feet first from a coma on the ground and back through the windshield frame, into her seat. She is singing Islands in the Stream on the radio. It sounds like backwards masking. Glass follows her and recollects in the windshield. Her eyes going from wide to relaxed. Her seatbelt reconnecting around her body. A can of cola unspills from my lap back into the can. A dog races back into the tree line. I notice and then I don't notice a guardrail.

I am coming Arianna.
I am drifting now.
A dark pool. My blood, moving out to my fingertips.
My blood, moving fast towards the light.
Arianna. Arianna. Arianna . Arianna. Arianna. Arianna. Arianna. Arianna.

Drown Him

I wished I hadn't yelled
at you. I never yell. That
specific brand of drink
made the bullhorn light up.
You were trying to be
funny. I was trying to whisper
in blue siren, in small dynamite,
in crimson teeth. I
thought his throat was dead,
suffocated in the stomach orchids.

It never died. I'm sorry. I'm sorry
my father's anger is mine.

As scared as you looked, this
is as I have always been. I have
been set straight by it. I knew
it would happen. I pretend it keeps
dying. How many funerals?

I walk fast at night. Something is
coming. Coming to take me.

I can't have kids. Loud kids.
I don't want to get into bed,
close my ears, and pretend
to die every night, and
pretend it died, every
night, and is finally over.

HUNTS WITH BOW

In a sporting goods store, a young man with a Carolina cash crop in his lip
helps me in the archery department.
I ask him what I need to begin the sport.

He says, *"Well, what do you want to kill?"*

I tell him, "I want to kill bales of hay. I have always hated hay."
No smile.
"Target practice, actually."

He said, *"Oh, you'll shoot through a bale of hay.
How long have you been using a hunting bow?"*

I told him I was just starting out.
He said, *"This compound bow
would be a good deer-hunting bow. You might as well go big
in case you feel like movin' on up in the food chain."*

I tell him, "Isn't it kind of amazing —
the boring life of a deer,
harming no one, and how it must die,
bleeding for hours with an arrow in it's ass when all it wanted
was to bend its head down and chew on something."

He says, *"It's natural.
Killing is natural.
All these hippies protesting war are still eating barbecue ribs."*

I nod and stand there looking at the picture of the deer on the bow case, unable
to visualize it bleeding out. Knowing if it were in front of me,
I would be fascinated to watch it die.

THE DESIRE OF MEMORY

When I was boy,
I wanted to grow up to be one of four things: stage magician,
invisible swamp creature, on the street newscaster, or fireman.

Couldn't imagine anything cooler than waking up and sliding down
a time-saving pole.

Quiet around others,
loud and alone in my head.
Plastic green tanks that were never the right scale.

I was hiding, often under the sink by the trash.
I couldn't smell things.
I was fine.

When I got older and hung out with the other kids,
I pretended to be interested in their lowered cars, their loud stereos,
and baseball statistics.
They would always ask,
"Derrick, can you do this? What can you do?"

What *could* I do?
I could learn four skateboard tricks
and not learn anymore.
I still know them. I'm steady.

When the kids pinned me down to throw matches in my hair
it wasn't because they hated me.
I thought they all had done it. They liked to burn everything.
I could weep in public.

I began making blowguns out of PVC pipe.
We threw lemons at the neighbor's garage door.
We didn't hate them.
We loved the sound.
We would steal Christmas light bulbs if they were the fat kind cause
    when you chucked them they would pop on impact with a loud
    BLOP!

We couldn't imagine buying something and wanting it to stay nice.

My toys and figurines were melted.
I wanted to blow up anything that would allow me.

Burn everything.

I got grounded for stripping a Barbie down to her smoothness.
I didn't know what a bikini area was supposed to look like
but I knew now that it looked like an unpeeled peach.

I was a
High school virgin on a scooter that went 30 mph. Lookout.
I was skinny and had a large head. I looked like a lollipop that fell in cat fur.

I got into magic.
My performances were often accompanied by Phil Collins hit track,
In the Air Tonight. It was on cassette. If I didn't stop the tape fast
enough at the end of the trick the track would cross fade into a super
neon jam called This Must Be Love. For my finale trick, zombie ball,
a silver ball magically floated atop a silk. A dove pan, full of flame, to
dove. The doves hated it.

At Knott's Berry Farm's magic shop.
I would wear a maroon vest and gray slacks with a dull clip on tie.
I would chase shoplifters in dress shoes.
I would make a fake tarantula drop from the ceiling
and land on someone's shoulder.
I would tell no one my secrets until they bought them.
I would make a room full of day campers say ooooooooooh.
I would wander the park after hours, imagining living
somewhere thought up.

Solid radio waves.
A graveyard on Mars.
The 2 legged dreams of copperhead snakes.
Love in a one person bed.
Disaster sex.
A book about my love of the smell of PVC pipe.

A newscaster's lounge.
A fireman's locker.
A swamp creature watching children outgrow him.
A magician turning his head
from the secret.

DRAMA

Mr. Baker was my Pacifica High School drama teacher.
He was bald, had Navy arms that could've killed me
and loved showtunes.

When handing out grades, he burst into a rage and
threw me across the room when I asked him
why I got a C and the girl who did nothing got an A.

The girl who got an A was darkwave quiet every day,
a solemn mascara party, very Siouxsie Sioux.
She dressed preppy on Halloween.

When I landed in the chairs I thought,
"I can't believe he threw me. In front of everyone.
I must now kill Mr. Baker.
I am 16 and I am going to kill a grown-up.
I wanna eat him face first."

Instead, I flew to the Principal's office like a Lark,
and he ran after me, cursing, "You little shit!"

In the Principal's office I said, "Mr. Wise,
Mr. Baker grabbed my arms and threw me into a pile of
chairs when I asked him why I got a low grade."

In a flurry, Mr. Baker lashed out into cussing rivets,
ready to murder my skinny.
The two adults were now yelling
at each other using each others first names.

I had never heard that before.

Mr. Wise was trying to calm and make sense.
Mr. Baker was trying to explain how I, or "little shit" had it coming
for pushing him over the edge.

At home, shaken, I asked my Mom if I should sue
and she said we weren't the suing type. She was right.

When spring break was over, I returned to class and Mr. Baker
was really pleasant to me.
Our eyes almost never met during lessons.

I realized I talked too much.
I knew I could hurt his career if I chirped.
I didn't like that feeling.
He was old, poorly dressed, and teaching drama in Garden Grove.

They transferred me to the kind and warm Mr. Marks' class.
I was the beast in Beauty and the Beast, Really.
The play made fun of the original musical.
I wore a mask and pretended that a young woman loved me,
and that I was sad to be an animal.

Mr. Baker came to the play I was in at the close of the long year.

He shook my hand.
He shook my parents' hands.
He came alone.
He told me I was going places.

The Bonfires of Pacific Coast Highway

The winds sweep, wild
gushes, makes everything talk.

The sundown, uneven
shutters, closes up shop.

The gust
prefers us
messy in dust.

I want to learn
how to say goodnight
with my whole body.

I drove CR and Karen along
the great slithering California highway.
We parked in Surf City, near the bird stained dock.

The wind sucked CR out to sea
and he came back with new blonde hair,
wet leather and a new song.

I asked him where new songs come from.
He pointed and said, "…out there, they're all out there.
Do I have urchin in my teeth?"

Karen had a lead dream fall out of her bag.
She was going to show me the heavy thing
she was carrying.

We just kicked some sand over it
and left
it behind.

We ate food in a kitchen
full of birds.
Karen ordered a bucket of pickles.

I said, "You can win folks over with sugar
more than vinegar, but sometimes vinegar is right.
Have another drink. Whiskey is wet sugar."

She said,
"Free whiskey
is sexual harassment." She still drank.

I took them to go see four rock bands in a strip mall.
One of the bands made the room smell like Christian sex.
Good skin. Light applause.

They were horrible and the place was packed for them.
If you don't go to church,
you will never have an automatic fan-base.

The flirty, worship looking lead singer lady asked me
if I had a girlfriend, I said, "I used to but her vagina looked like
an old man eating... so it's over."

I only said this to make my friends laugh.
Karen giggled and shook
her head like an etch-a-sketch.

The other band sounded like Interpol.
Even Interpol
tries to not sound like Interpol.

The last band uttered the worst
thing anyone has ever heard at any show,
"I just wanna thank you guys for coming out tonight. Goodnight, God Bless."

No one means it. It always falls out the mouth like balls in short-shorts.
Even, "Thank you for listening to our shitty passion"
is three thousand leagues better.

Why not say something good?
Let goodnight be
valuable.

"Whip cream is angel turd. Goodnight."
"People who wear Tom's shoes are bad in bed. Goodnight."
"Start an all-gay, all-seafood bar called fish and chaps. Goodnight."

 "Tenderloin and smegma are the worst words. Goodnight."
"You are no longer wearing a bra, you are wearing a night bikini! Goodnight."
"Churros are just donuts with boners. Goodnight."

"Free whiskey
is sexual harassment.
Goodnight."

We drove back through the midnight bonfire smoke and spray
of the Pacific to our tiny beds. CR said, "Guys, I have laughed up a song
called, 'Goodnight with Your Whole Body.'"

He just howled and shook around,
like an idiot
with a junebug problem.

All sand and song flowed from his teeth.
Karen scooped it back into his mouth, tipped him over like an
        hourglass and said,
"Sing again. Sing this night into memory. This was Goodnight."

POEM FOR THE LEAPING GHOST

There is nothing overly sentimental
in telling another man you love him,
but I have often squirmed at fatherly love.
It has been there since I thought God
was waiting for me to show up.

Russ, these are short numbers we dance.
In the quiet of our stories, there is always looking back.
How strange, looking backwards makes you feel
like you're being chased.

I hope the good memories chase you in the smoke and palm trees of
    night.

The bad ones that try to jam up your light, they deserve room, but no
    voice.

Sometimes your stories, Russ, are as long as a yearbook. I sometimes
stop listening and imagine your heart is Gargantua, overflowing with
booze-blood and black and white cinema strobes. It is as plump as
your brush. Passionate as a young fuck.

I see you as tarantula tamer. Horror strainer. You are not a snapping
Jet/ Shark basher. You are not a wild doctor, not a Dracula killer,
not a malty sea Captain, not a wide eyed priest, not an old God, not
the bewildered love interest, not the drug, not the small flex in the
minute hand.

You are the spittle and dust of now and as I look at you, I'm trying
to recall exactly what I will recall about you. You were never what
people want to remember you as. They might know you and the
greatness of a moment you captured in your films, but I wish they
could see you in this bar, cracking everyone up.

You made it to now. That is the big deal. That is everything. If you
feel like shit, you blew it. I doubt you do. You lived your ass off and
have not been throat kicked by your mistakes. You sang. You still
sing.

You ran the sprint and you loved 'til your pants split into surrender rags and you yelled 'til your tongue went limp, and you rolled and danced gold nugget sweat, and loved by force, and they saw it. They saw you ball-peen hammer through this life. You mellowed through the flickering storm. You are the lead. Toss out. Step change. I see it now too. A kind of laugh can be a kind of love, schmaltzy or not.

You ain't dead. That's something. That's nice. The other thing is nice too. Ain't love a simple motherfucker? It is the ghost we can chase, lock or shove. Ain't it good to leap into the arms of the audience? You listen to us young punks and our unchiseled stories. You become the audience.

We talk of how some never leap. They too are loved.

Maybe not as brightly.

JOY IN PLACES WITHOUT YOU

Northfield, Minnesota is pastel quiet,
is without your strut,
your lovely saffron gust and mint smoke.

I am glad you are not here. Northfield is smell.

On the east side, in the Malto-meal plant
they're making thousands of boxes
of knock-off breakfast cereals that sound like bad love tricks:
Tootie Fruities, Coco-roos, Honey Nut Scooters, Corn Bursts,
Blueberry Muffin Tops, Nut Buzzers, Golden Puffs,
and coming soon, Cheerful Circles.

I'd love to walk into the office,
barefoot and hollering
that I bit into a cheerful circle.

On the west side,
they're slicing the softest turkey necks,
cutting off the feathery haunches,
melting down the gluey bones.

The sorrowful smell collision goes right into my Lager.
I am drinking the greatest slaughter this season. The smell is becoming me.

I am here at the rube-n-stein pub
making this for you.
This cheap photography,
warp and scribble.

Slow and warm in the birch walls
under the dumb paintings,
the TV sound, the famous TV light,
showing people falling off of chairs and an audience dressed like Mormons,
laughing like someone told them to.

The smell I miss is you, the thing I become.
Yes, I know it is the worst thing to say to a lover:

I miss all your smells.
I ponder what they really are
cause they aren't impossible saffron, or new lemons, or cinnamon sex mix.

It could just be soap. I miss your soap.
I can't name it. Why do tears come?

I believe I am happy
and don't
know what to do with it.

I'll let it all slide down my face
and drop onto my tongue.
I sing the words:
How will I ever go back from here?

THE MOST POETIC POEM
an ars poetica
in the key of Alicia

Someone like me, after sipping absinthe and blind pacifism said,
"Bombing for peace is like screwing for virginity."

The same is now true for authors.
"Writing about poetry is like shitting about toilets."

I won't write a poem about poetry
because poetry is search and capture
and reading about poetry is like watching your wife
talk about shopping when you wish she would just shop.

Jotting down all
that the gods won't let you have:
— A stockroom full of voluntarily nude and softball-attractive
    derby girls from around the world that you get to serve beef
    jerky and elbows to, calling it Voltaire.

— A keg of magic beer near the fire pole in your tree house, and
    when you drink it you mysteriously say dumb shit about the
    nightmoon, an aardvarks heart, and foot fancy.

— A New Jersey that someday smells less like rental shoes.

— A zebra farm in winter that reminds you of all bar codes
    running away, a society that doesn't refer to itself as society.

— Finding your poetry voice and catching her making money on
    the side at a second-guessing gig, wishing up a novel.

If you write a poem about poetry
you really do
become part of the pro
blem.

What a Room!

Look at the energy blurtzing across this room!
Oh how it blooms.
Why bother swooping
when you can swoon?

Why feel fine
when you can feel find?
Why fall in love
when you can climb?

This room is hereby fortified
with the cleansing power
of the states greatest lovers
lurking with powder
burns.

Get some cream on that mess! Put a dime in your penny loafers!

Aloha, hello is goodbye
and goodbye is pineapple toodle-loo.
Goodbye lame lows.
Goodbye performance shits.
Goodbye orchestra of pride,
that blithering death trance
of tight lips and fingered valves.
I eat your instruments
and detonate this sonata fuck spree.

I am new music. I am spoon shining in the jungle.
Jungle spoon! I want to scoop!
If you dress like a trailer, we will get hitched.

Let's get married as conservatives do.
Let's get drunk and have a bed wedding.
Let's bury old photos and make light bloom.
Let's rob a blood bank with no pants on screaming, "This
is a stick up. Way up! We brought candy.
We are the only robbers who bring you things!"

I need your imagination to wash the dead out of me.

I accidentally put all my dirty laundry in the wishing machine.
The dryer opened on its own.
It was everything I ever lost. Even Heather.
An unpaid plane ticket stuck to her clean face. Dizzy. Too Dry.
Warm against my head.

Then an empty penny loafer. A jungle print blanket.
It's everything I ever lost. Even Wendy. Smelling like softener.
I wanted it laid out on my bed. I wanted to sleep under it all.

A telegram from far away is stuck to a sock. It says:

THE WOMEN YOU WANT TO LOVE ARE MARRIED. STOP.
YOU LOOK UGLY WHEN YOU SING. STOP.
THERE IS A WOMAN, WITH A LAZARUS VOICE AND
SHE WILL RAISE IT FOR YOU.

Telling her I loved her was like yelling underwater.
Couldn't hear it, but said she could see it.
The heart beat in a drippy faucet, the flickering bulbs,
       —the dirty lost things, the room. Our room.
            Oh, how it blooms.
            Oh, how it blooms.

SWITCHBLADE MERMAID

Look at how my hair lifts when the air is filled
and thunder arrives.

You
charged my
skin
with a
horrible weather.

I was underdressed.

There are no questions
in the hands I
write around you.

I do not wish for a tiny microphone
on the back of your little licorice throat.
Let the secrets in your satin heart settle down.
Let that heart blaze, how it can jealous the sunset.

I do not wonder what lifts the soft blonde
on your sleek four track neck.
I do not wonder where your eyes bonfire
when the pounding rises in the woods.

I do not wonder what knives you have held
in your good teeth.
I can tell they were sharp. Sides of your mouth.

I do not wonder what mad God made your breasts
jubilee worthy. Parade city.
I do not wonder about the science class boner beauty.
Your Gold is soft.
I do not wonder of the perfect Persian plaster
your legs were blasted from.

I know it every night
on sleep's great blurry projector.

The slumbering man
filled with dinner hammers
and failure hammers and a hunger
to fix
without ever been given
the right tools.

I will mess you up. You are coat.
I will wear you out.

When we touch
it is salt that leaves.

We cannot live without salt.
We are not living if we don't burn it away
to find more.

Oh, furious love,
I can still hear you.

And when you are still
I can hear you more.

The Last Weatherman

The weatherman lives a life of no poetry.

"Science holds no imagination to beauty.

Science is all that is real."

He performs his final run through before the regular evening taping, muttering the phrases: "Partial Clouds…Hail among thunderstorms…High pressure system… a pusssssh of energy moves into the region…"

His life is control.
His life is a table for one, always able to find a seat at the movies.
Tandem bikes make him vomit. Someone is always pulling someone's weight.

His desk at work is dominated by "the small dogs in big shirts" calendar and a dumb coffee cup.

At home, there are no plants. Why take care of something that tries to die if you ignore it?
His kitchen is just a place to stand sometimes. Someone he doesn't know sent him a package so he didn't open it. It feels like a book. "No thanks." His bed has one pillow. No one believes it but the weatherman is as happy as he is.

Something peculiar happened during the regular evening taping.

"And… speed."

"And we're back now with our Accuweather Forecast, what's going on out there in those wild skies of ours?"

"I'm glad you asked Lea because we have some heavy tzz bundling up to do this weekend due to another high pressure sister… pushing it's way like a frag-tzzzlgrp freak caboose… full of PCP. Precipi..PCP. Sorry. I'll pickup… and rolling…A strong thunderstrum of brain and blaze of hell, pure hell falling to the refreshed, a harbor for the forgotten..tzzzglpn forecast-in, cave in… Hail, my will, my tzzz cave…tllzzzgnp. Hup. Can I retake that?"

That was the day it started. The day his words fought their way out of his mouth.

He walks to work every morning. The sky is only blue. The clouds are a good white.
The coffee is just hot.

He looks at the picture of someone he once knew on his desk.
The day the words took over was the first day he noticed anything small.
The picture used to tell him, "I don't need you to be love, I need you to be a solution." Something strange happened.
He noticed his coffee mug for the first time.
The smooth handle.
The stains on the inside lip.
The dumb 'coffee makes me poop' slogan.

He never thought it was beautiful before today, but he started to think about beautiful holding devices and his mind began to exhale, after a full life of inhaling.

A homeless man outside the studio asks him
what the weather is going to be like.
"If ya get a chance, tune in. We need more viewers."

He plays a broken toy piano. Old green cut off military gloves. Today the homeless man says, "*Give me some insight brother. I gotta find shelter tonight or what?? Don't tell me to tune in or I'll eat your mouth.*"

The weatherman tried to summon a sensible response
but all that came out was,
"Well, thunderstrums, a blaze of hell.
I don't know what tzzz going on!"

He said, "*Holy moly. It found you!*"

"What found me?"

"*The bad weather of words, buttmugger. You needed it too.
You a big ugly vase and all ya flowers is dead.
The bad weather of words commands us to celebrate and spin.*

Consider the battered piñata.
They may beat you to bits, but there's still some good candy inside.
You just got to shake it around.
Notice the living. You need to spaz-bonfire.
The bad weather of words tells you to burn like Watts,
before the riots, when the fire was building inside people first—
Is a hard brain gonna fall?"

"Yes."

"I'll find shelter. When I get too wet,
I have to go home and change. Enjoy the burn freak caboose!"

It was the day words found him,
His lips were like wet 9-volt batteries.
His lungs shrank and his breathing turtled
as his heart grew away from its old scuttled shell.
His break room ice cream melted, as it should, but it was not a mess,
it was officially a chance to lick his hand. He even threw it into the
air and tried to lick it on the way down. The mess was new.

The weatherman tried to warm up
for the Saturday evening taping. It all came out as:

(1) There is going to be a tasty solid chill in the air, lets do the
penguin belly glide on it.

(2) The oncoming humidity is going to unbutton every denim blouse
and unzip every costume.

(3) Set your windshield wipers to gospel high yi yi!

(4) The wind is so calm you will want to whisper back 'I missed you'
in fake French. Lefondle. Du swoosh ette.

(5) We have a stampede of storms on radar. I shall ride it for nine
seconds!

It was exhausting, but Saturday night finally ended
the way the weatherman had secretly wished it would,
like a good poem—unexpected, a warm quiet.

It ended like moonlight into the ground.

So here's to punching holes in the ceiling and waiting for the stars to suck. Here's to the bad weather of words finding you, to the nails in the black air being pulled out by the passionate claw hammer, the night sky blanketing down upon us in jet black silk and octopus ink.

Here's to the thunderstrums and your oncoming blaze of hell.

"If you are cooking something in the kitchen tonight,
slow down and see the meal in the pot.
Notice the pot.
Maybe leave the meal in the sauce longer.
Look out the window.

A high pressure sister is definitely coming our way."

THE SECRET

I went on a date to the Belmont Pier and brought
an old dying cell phone.

I found it in my cedar chest.
I don't know whose phone number was in it
that made me want to keep it.
I couldn't get it to work,
but the screen did turn on
and the text said, "Hello."

Dusk drifted in. I gave her my jacket.
Drank Malbec in the parking lot, listened to cassettes
of old radio shows on a tiny boom box. She closed
her eyes when she laughed. Lovely.

Her friend, pre-show, told me that she preferred impulsive men.
I just happened to have impulse in my pocket.

We walked along the battered planks.
Cargo ships and cabin lights.
Buoys baritone horning.

Discussing citronella and the positive impact of
a talented Foley artist. Her lips were Japanese camellia.

I told her I had to take a call.
After the "call" was over, I said:
"You know, that was rude.
I can't believe I'm numb to it.
I'm with you, nervous,
and not allowing myself to be in this moment.
I feel like I fill up all the down time with the unreal, like
I gain speed from technology but lose slow,
beautiful moments and meaningful interaction.
I apologize. You're stunning.
Damn it all."

I chucked my phone out to sea.

Her eyes startled their sugars
into me and then below as she watched
the light from the phone, fading
like a drifting astronaut.

The birds, floating and dumb.
The soft seaweed breeze.

The water went dark again and
she kissed me. I couldn't wait to hold onto her face again.

After dropping her off after midnight, driving towards home,
I can't tell you how I had wished, with all my guts,
that I was smart enough to not have
answered her call.

STRANGE LIGHT

0- dark.

0- voice.

Here is the story of a man with strange light
and tiny blisses.

A story of wild me lost among wild you.
I wanted to be down
in the obscene with you.
I wanted to see it all.
To leave the black, slow sea
of the heavens.
Here is how pure and empty peace can be.
Days with no end—navigating celestially. Bored to life.

I wanted to be with you.
To taste warm blue
waves of deep salt.

The council asked me why I wanted to descend
into the territory
of those gloriously unplugged buzzards.

I told them I wanted the song of horrible, amazing.
The plush rest of joy.
The sensations of the spirit mended and becoming aware.
To writhe among the living things.
To holler among the public.

To holler under the afternoon rainstorm juice.
To cheer on that tornado ballet
and finally let it all out.
To watch the house lift away
and feel better, tornado.
To feel the kiss of a drunk dog and say, "I know."

To hunt God.
To wash the mud from my gun after finding him
hiding in the soil.
To put his bloodied head on my wall.

To hunger in my veins for a No trophy life.
No trophy love.

To succeed at floating
when people urge me to sink.
To fail at hotel bed diving.
To fall for the night buzz and sudden bugs
of writing, that cheap photography.
To smell smoke nearby when I am cold.
To grieve the way I couldn't imagine grieving.
To grieve alone
and feel my muscles growing from it.

To have one choice and choose poorly.
To be thrown from the car crash and wait in the tree-line,
listening to crickets trying to call for help for me.
I can see it all.

To undo the face of my enemy.
To love them silently.
To aim my lung cannons for fascination
and burst into viola.
The mouth is clarinet, is pipe bomb,
the ears, open wounds,
these piano songs, bandages.

I want to have sunlight learn me,
to learn my shape.
I want to learn why a bomb sings only
one note
as it falls through the air.
It is breaking the air.
I want to break against the air.
Just let me down.
I am ready to wrap my future arms around it all.

I am ready to dance
wolf-skinny under the bald moon.
The egg shell moon.
The quarter moon that looks like an Arabic shoe.
That beat-up moon,
lifting higher like a balloon from a child's buttery hands.
The looming, foaming, moon,
tired of being written down or dreamily discussed,
I want to know why it returns and who it returns for.
I want to invent why,
the answer, gleaming across me.

To hold the nervous hand of my love and then
watch their hair turn beautiful as they walk away.

To marvel at young unwanted boners.
That random bullhorn in the trousers.

To welcome light as the next shift.
To watch it slip away and not know much.
To wonder about it all and know that it was good.
To know that it was good and it was all.

To marvel at the journey of impossible lovers.

To notice the trophy missing from my wall
and know that God can be found and escape.

To see our weaknesses.

For all this is worthy of experience.
The experience of undoing and becoming.
To be.

A plea.

I fell to Earth and saw what Lucifer saw
on his way down,
and it was beautiful enough to break
even the blackest of hearts.

0-dark.

0-dark.

1-on.

Born as a small surprise of light. Low-budget Christmas tree light.
I had a heart full of volume and grizzly bear drool.
A loud little spaz. Born hollering and all gooped up.

I made it! I made it! I'm here! I'm here, you HUGE fuckers!
                    I don't know anything but this hollering!
I wasn't yelling in English.
It was babe-lish, relish, power babble.

Nothing could shut my brass mouth up.

My cries meant: I miss the womb,
I didn't know that I didn't know how to do anything!
Swinging my limbs in the air like a messy idiot.
Someone cry out that your boy is born!
My mother relieved to have the blob out of her. Proud as peach pie.
When I was born, my father jumped around like barefoot summer concrete.
        Our harmony of uncontrollable screaming: *my boy is born—*
my boy's born and no one gets to touch it... touch him.

*Oh my Lord, Oh my Lord. I have a suitcase full of all the things I could not
be. I can not wait to dress him in all of it!*

My light was that of my mother's and it was bright and correct.
It was.

3- On Dad's shoulders.
4- I hit a kid with a croquet mallet.
6- Penguins humping at the zoo

When I was young I was dressed in the wrong clothes.
The holes in my jeans were advent calendars.
I was afraid a lot.
Afraid of the devil chasing me in my dreams and helicopters...
with devils in them! And lasers. Bad lasers.

I was afraid of the dark.
My father was red lights and tall blue grass.
I was afraid of getting the punishment
of the swinging belt in the dark.
I was afraid of pulling down my pants and getting the belt
the wooden spoon, the plum branch, the belt buckle in the dark,
not knowing when the swing was coming, or where it would make contact.
My father would say, "don't you ever do that again"
Swinging with each "ever."
Fury coloring his skin in rubies.
I wonder when rage first bit his ankles
and filled his Texas blood.
I wonder why it doesn't find me.
I wonder if it is waiting.

I know that when I am older, I don't want kids —
maybe so there is no one for me to unload and rev upon.

I'll marry the dark.
When the dark comes I will party in it.
I will make it silly.
I will keep my light.

I wrote to him last year,
that I wanted to know his life.
Asked him if he was dating, and how his back was.
He wrote back,
"May God richly bless you..." It had an ellipses.
As if he was going to add, "...for me, he did not,
or you know what they say..."

Grief had stolen many of his words.

I see him as a man who tried
and is tired of the trying.
A man with bags and bags of ellipses.
I could not fit in his clothes.
His days are waiting for things to grow dim,
wondering if this is what he was made for,
the end, pulling him like a cable.

I sleep in the day.

The belts I see in stores are something to me now,
small noose, devil's tail,
horse whipped to death.
I try to fill my head with Christmas.

I asked for a telescope for Christmas
so I could see far from this place.

A place to wait for rain
or any kind of storm.
A tornado that removes everything.
I hear him sometimes.
"...except for you and your sister, I dunno...."

10 - Rode my bike into a washing machine and lived.
11- Started saying the word shit, comfortably.
14- Got the shit kicked out of me.

One day, when I felt as alone as Hawaii-
I decided I didn't want to be afraid anymore.
I was getting close to teen-hood, lankier and feeling different,
like one tasty pear in a pile of pomegranates.
At school they tried to tell me:

DON'T DO ANYTHING DIFFERENT!
DON'T DO ANYTHING DANGEROUS OR FRILLY!
DON'T SEARCH TOO FAR OR YOU WILL BE BURIED!
DON'T REVEAL THAT WHICH IS SCARY!
and a few teachers cried:

but
the kids got heart
the kids got heart
the kids got heart
let him out
no no no no

stand up
up straight

straight back
hold still
fashion lips tight
soften the voice,
unhard your stare
mind manners
tuck your derriere
fair skin
no muscle
gas face
no seconds
little boy
little boy
stop crying for water

the kids got heart
but the kids got heart
no no no no no !

submissive turkey legs, chicken arms
his face looks like animal hell
what a fashion collapse
perm your curly brain
sit suck down
back straight black nape
clean your neck
wash your ass
chin up, chow down
hold still cradle, cradle
sit up straight
stand like a man, stand like a plant
never tell a lie
just keep inventing answers
stop crying for water
stop dreaming of dancers
lifting you away

but the kids got heart
no no no no

He thought Jesus' blood was diet coke!
Don't talk in rewind
Don't eat phone
Don't bite table, boy!
Your rough can be honed
Don't vomit light
Don't kiss the engine when it is running
Don't draw visions of death on your final exam
or stare at its entrance, smiling
Don't get gashey or outspin throwing knives
Don't show off, don't show on, don't Chopin! Don't Gershwin!

But doesn't the kid got heart?
No No No!

There does seem to be something revving unnatural.
It may be an elephant on a bicycle,
something big and overly handled
inside this little puke.
It may be losing its balance,
not saying it's too big,
it's just elaborate.
Something elaborate inside this puke.
It will never do.

The kid has heart! The crowd screams.
It's best we let him loose.
"Let go or be dragged."
A waterskier on a skateboard
being towed behind a fast moving car.
Whaaaa! Oh shit city.

Ahhh. Maybe we send him into the imploding zoo of the metropolis.
Where he can get more lost,
commanding the street lights.
Let him scream spazzfucky unto those golden beams,
befriending the archers in the shadows, cleaning his ears
with the harmless ends of arrows,
hearing all the rules wrong,
doomed with the wasted and poor,

hearing the hum of desire,
the air filters of cooling imagination—
jotting it all down for what?
No manners.
No success.
No timing.
What if he becomes nothing?

He does have heart,
and that is only worth a glass of water.
Give him a drink. Let him go.
What a puke. What a black bag
of unknown fantastic.

18- Kissed a girl in a play and wanted to be in every play.

19- Received paratrooper medal for excellence with grenade
launcher.

22- Drove cross country alone.

24- Tried to write a long poem. It was almost a full page. Double
spaced.

In my twenties, I was army,

then I was lonely as museum treasure,

then I was free.

In the great outside, she found me.
She was wearing too many colors to be taken seriously.
I was in my 20's and posing like Hemingway's valet.
Calling Paris and telling it was over.
Drinking and wishing I knew how to fight with my pants down.
Wondering how to claw my way into a dress
since "talent" wasn't working.
Proud of my dim light. The dimming

Margaret wasn't afraid of anything. Lonely too, but not tragic.

She didn't trust anyone barefoot.

Her heart had no crust.
She smelled like jasmine off the vine and new books.
A woman born with a capacity for sunbursting.
Hair of dirty tinsel, brown and furious.
Her hands were branding irons and I soon became hers.
Off to the park with a flask full of anesthesia.
The snails rolled up inside their shells,
rocking back and forth against each other.
This was a glossy summer and everything was in love.

Our hearts spread eagle and searched, thoroughly.
I had never heard the word splendor come out of a girl's mouth before.
I heard it when she was asleep.
She told me she still saw something flickering in me
and that it was enough to keep her warm.
We ain't star-crossed, We are horny music.
We are the scorn of the boring.

What kind of woman draws a survival manual for the wilderness
in case humans attacked her?

Spiders don't feel scary around her. They told me.
She longs for the ocean to freeze so we can slide to Ghana.

A falcon dives at 200 mph.
A human can run up to 27 miles per hour.
I am slow love.
I move at the speed of bad mood lighting.
She still moved towards my poverty and loved me for years.

I loved her with all my heart.
I loved her with all of everyone's heart.
I won't love you forever Margaret.
But I will love you with all of my weird might
for as long as the day will allow.
Everything is supposed to die. It doesn't frighten me now.

26 -Lived in the mountains. Grew a beard and it didn't make me
    smart.

27- Lived in the desert. It was a dry boring.

30- Lived on a boat. Loved Margaret in a crazy fashion.

I first time I saw Margaret's body and I did not know what to do with it.
Then all of a sudden… I did know what to do with it.
I did not know what it would do to me.
It did it to me, right and full on.

Our breath, shoving.

Our lips, doin' the light blossom.

A woman in a bra is like seeing a hammer nailed to a wall.
I had pants full of nails and lots of fixin' to do.

She crosses her legs and keeps crossing them
until she is wound up.
I blow on her windward side
and she spins into the ground like a cement drill.

I see her pink dregs,
her fast healing,
her righteous sweet potatoes,
her knees and ankles in knots.
She is nervous, marvelous, deep in the dirt.
Winding up and unwinding like a sweater
that cannot make up its mind.
I felt loose as hell and it was good.
She was porn for dead girls.
She was a fridge full of synthetic blood
in a reckless town.

I think of birds now.
I imagine the worms' last sensation as it lifts up into the air,
feeling its first breeze while flying
in the ravens mouth. *This is nice, I wish…chomp.*
That is pretty close to how she made me feel,
without the *chomp*,
but a wonder when the chomp would come.
Will you fade Margaret?
Like a magazine left in the sunlit window?
I cannot unlace you from my head.

She gave her days to me and we flowered into years.

32- Started rowing boats for a living.

34- Started screwing in weird places, locations that is.

36- Someone tried to stab me in London. I won.

NOW

The literal now is very insecure.

Age 38, dressed poorly for going out, in ...
a comfortably air conditioned theater in, HowdidIgethere, Holland,
maybe, terrified of good reviews and still standing with his heart in
    low dazzle.
I'm worried about standing over there because that is 39,
and over there a little further is 40,
and it is too hard to see if those numbers make sense.
The narrator is wondering if anyone in the front row will share his or
    her drink
because he has been working his ass off.

40- We never married. I knocked over a water cooler at work. I was
    hit by fireworks.

44- My back got weak. Disability. I tried painting. I was terrible. I
    became terrible.

48-We parted. I miss her. I'm glad she is gone, for her sake.

49- I dunno.

I step heavy as any older man,

I have a dream about walking backwards through devastation,
a destroyed place,
realizing at the end of the poem that I did it.
The great news is that I could see things growing
once the soil had been tilled by my explosions.
There were signs littered about, no loitering and such. They said:

No proof
No baster
No finger twitch
No soft metal station
No yellowing in the eyes
No sissy strut
No bowler's sag
No shoes repaired
No burning fire escape
No wedding march with sirens
No fever pros
No rosy funeral
No brawl for your tits
No reason to hold your fingernails in your teeth
No staying power for things in flight
No binocular peep show
No day nakedness
No lust laid upon you like your favorite jacket
No cloud cover Sunday
No shade in the desert
No water spout at sea
No black smokers below
No signs of the end
No signs on the road
No end
No markings on the road
No now

I'm 49
The night is coming, the great night, falling slow and easy.
I'm 57
The night moves towards me like a coffin on a luggage carousel.
I'm 68
The night is always possible. Margaret's funeral was poorly put
    together. The food was awful.
I'm 72
I am tired.
73
I cannot die. Margaret.

No pine tar heart!
No costume armor parade!
No graceful widows walk!
No sissy strut soft metal!
no hard star glimmer in my eye
no white light dream sequence.
Fuck you death.
No sequin sorrow shining from me.
Hurrah these ghostly places.
Hurrah, hurrah the drunk calligraphy of two bodies unfurling in my mind.
Margaret, Margaret,
your nervous laughter feels like home.
I sing of your sudden lust,
your ease in fumbling for the things
I could never retrieve.
Every mansion in this town is bored,
including heaven's.
All their closets full of shiny skeletons.
They will never play our music.
They can keep all the smelly pearls in those gates.
I must keep you alive in my head Margaret.
I loved your full resume.
I loved your throaty kiss.
I am gushing and I am scared.
I am ready to fill this night with senseless acts of
ha cha cha.
I'm going berzerker.
I ain't goin west
like death,
I am still a tornado ballet.
Hurrah, hurrah us loyal dogs!
Hurrah, hurrah the echo that is not forever.
Hurrah, hurrah the things that do not last.
Hurrah, hurrah the night, the naked, and the poor
floating upon it.
I don't want my story to be held hostage,
I want it to be haunted. Spooky and true.
I want chance to flow in through the windows like a flood.
I cannot will this poem into life.

This is what it wanted to say to you Margaret.
Did I do the poem right? Did I?
This is more. This is all of it.
I am sorry for wanting what I was, what we were
and I know you are sorry for wanting that too.

I tried to blow my chest out
with a flashlight,
searing out the hearts chunky mess
to find you, and there you are, still holding me.
The Luminous Margaret.
I will not fear the night, but
is this you?
Is this you pulling me to you?

The tar pits of love,
come suck me in.
All hail the ships
that sail beyond dusk, without wind.
To navigate blindly.
All love is love in the dark.
To hang on long enough to say,
I'm sorry. The no poetry of I'm sorry.

I am coming home.

When we die
it is poetry
that leaves
the body.

Derrick Brown's Famous Last Words

Here, hold my watch.

That's probably only 80 or 90 feet down according to my spit test.

I'm 74% positive that's the guy.

This looks as fresh as possible. Dig in.

I've gotten down lots of feral cats from trees.

If it starts to growl, you go for help and I'll distract it.

Do I just swallow it, or do I have to bite down to kill it first?

Is that all the wasabi you got back there?

I should probably take my shirt off for this.

ABOUT THE AUTHOR

As one of the most original and well-traveled writer/performers in the country, Derrick Brown has gained a cult following for his poetry performances all over the U.S. and Europe. A poetic terrorism group has taken to tagging his metaphors across the globe. About.com called his former collection, *Scandalabra*, one of the best books of 2009.

To date, Brown has performed at over 1500 venues and universities internationally including The Tonight Show with Jay Leno, La Sorbonne in Paris, CBGB's in NYC, The Aquarium of The Pacific, All Tomorrows parties with the Flaming Lips and David Cross and a small Jewish youth group in Glendale. He is the president of Write Bloody Publishing so getting this book accepted was a breeze. He lives at sea in Long Beach, CA.

brownpoetry.com

NOTES

"Strange Light" was commissioned by Stephen Shropshire and The Noord Nederlandse Dance Group, Holland.

Dedications:

"Poem for The Leaping Ghost" is for Russ Tamblyn

"Joy in Places Without You" is for Jessica Blakeley

"Bonfires of PCH" is for Karen Finneyfrock and CR Avery

"I Hate You" is for that Grade A, A-hole, Anis Mojgani

"Vocoder Mango" is for Gabrielle Dunkeley

"Drama" is for Mr. Ken Marks

"The Last Weatherman" is for Sports Reporter Joel Chmara and Garden Wizard Buddy Wakefield

"Unacceptance Speech" is for Mindy Nettifee

"Hunts With Bow" is for The Great State of Tennessee

"Famous Last Words" is for Daniel Lisi, the man who cannot die.

Special Revving Thank You's to the wonderful Reba Jean Ney, Caitlin Moe, Cristin O'keefe Aptowicz, Lea Deschenes, Buzzy Enniss, Stephanie Bassos, Teen Liu, Rachel Brown, Lilly, Ali, Beth Lisick, Bingham, Grimeys, Open, Fingerprints, Josh Grieve, Shea Sizzle, Mr Figler, Andy Buell, Emily Wells, Timmy Straw, Mr. Wakefield, Mr. Mojgani, Cold War Kids, Havilah, Jeffrey McDaniel, Jeremy Radin, Joel Chmara, Germany, Angry Sam, Kevin Sampsell, Ma and Pa, Sarnowski, Howze, Rebecca Gillespie, Ross and Heidi, Sara Mitchell, Trinity, Mcgoo and Tristan Silverman.

NEW WRITE BLOODY BOOKS FOR 2011

Dear Future Boyfriend
Cristin O'Keefe Aptowicz's debut collection of poetry tackles
love and heartbreak with no-nonsense honesty and wit.

38 Bar Blues
C. R. Avery's second book, loaded with bar-stool musicality and brass-knuckle poetry.

Workin' Mime to Five
Dick Richard is a fired cruise ship pantomimist. You too can learn
his secret, creative pantomime moves. Humor by Derrick Brown.

Reasons to Leave the Slaughter
Ben Clark's book of poetry revels in youthful discovery from the heartland
and the balance between beauty and brutality.

Birthday Girl with Possum
Brendan Constantine's second book of poetry examines the invisible lines
between wonder & disappointment, ecstasy & crime, savagery & innocence.

Yesterday Won't Goodbye
Boston gutter punk Brian Ellis releases his second book of poetry,
filled with unbridled energy and vitality.

Write About an Empty Birdcage
Debut collection of poetry from Elaina M. Ellis that flirts with loss,
reveres appetite, and unzips identity.

These Are the Breaks
Essays from one of hip-hops deftest public intellectuals, Idris Goodwin

Bring Down the Chandeliers
Tara Hardy, a working-class queer survivor of incest, turns sex,
trauma and forgiveness inside out in this collection of new poems.

1,000 Black Umbrellas
The first internationally released collection of poetry
by old school author Daniel McGinn.

The Feather Room
Anis Mojgani's second collection of poetry explores storytelling and
poetic form while traveling farther down the path of magic realism.

Love in a Time of Robot Apocalypse
Latino-American poet David Perez releases his first book
of incisive, arresting, and end-of-the-world-as-we-know-it poetry.

The New Clean
Jon Sands' poetry redefines what it means to laugh, cry, mop it up and start again.

Sunset at the Temple of Olives
Paul Suntup's unforgettable voice merges subversive surrealism
and vivid grief in this debut collection of poetry.

Gentleman Practice
Righteous Babe Records artist and 3-time International Poetry Champ
Buddy Wakefield spins a nonfiction tale of a relay race to the light.

How to Seduce a White Boy in Ten Easy Steps
Debut collection for feminist, biracial poet Laura Yes Yes
dazzles with its explorations into the politics and metaphysics of identity.

Hot Teen Slut
Cristin O'Keefe Aptowicz's second book recounts stories of
a virgin poet who spent a year writing for the porn business.

Working Class Represent
A young poet humorously balances an office job with the life
of a touring performance poet in Cristin O'Keefe Aptowicz's third book of poetry

Oh, Terrible Youth
Cristin O'Keefe Aptowicz's plump collection commiserates and celebrates
all the wonder, terror, banality and comedy that is the long journey to adulthood.

OTHER WRITE BLOODY BOOKS (2003 - 2010)

Great Balls of Flowers (2009)
Steve Abee's poetry is accessible, insightful, hilarious, compelling,
upsetting, and inspiring. TNB Book of the Year.

Everything Is Everything (2010)
The latest collection from poet Cristin O'Keefe Aptowicz,
filled with crack squirrels, fat presidents, and el Chupacabra.

Catacomb Confetti (2010)
Inspired by nameless Parisian skulls in the catacombs of France,
Catacomb Confetti assures Joshua Boyd's poetic immortality.

Born in the Year of the Butterfly Knife (2004)
The Derrick Brown poetry collection that birthed Write Bloody Publishing.
Sincere, twisted, and violently romantic.

I Love You Is Back (2006)
A poetry collection by Derrick Brown.
"One moment tender, funny, or romantic, the next, visceral, ironic,
and revelatory—Here is the full chaos of life." (Janet Fitch, *White Oleander*)

Scandalabra (2009)
Former paratrooper Derrick Brown releases a stunning collection of poems written
at sea and in Nashville, TN. About.com's book of the year for poetry

Don't Smell the Floss (2009)
Award-winning writer Matty Byloos' first book of bizarre, absurd, and deliciously
perverse short stories puts your drunk uncle to shame.

The Bones Below (2010)
National Slam Champion Sierra DeMulder performs and teaches
with the release of her first book of hard-hitting, haunting poetry.

The Constant Velocity of Trains (2008)
The brain's left and right hemispheres collide in Lea Deschenes' Pushcart-Nominated
book of poetry about physics, relationships, and life's balancing acts.

Heavy Lead Birdsong (2008)
Award-winning academic poet Ryler Dustin releases his most
definitive collection of surreal love poetry.

Uncontrolled Experiments in Freedom (2008)
Boston underground art scene fixture Brian Ellis
becomes one of America's foremost narrative poetry performers.

Ceremony for the Choking Ghost (2010)
Slam legend Karen Finneyfrock's second book of poems ventures
into the humor and madness that surrounds familial loss.

Pole Dancing to Gospel Hymns (2008)
Andrea Gibson, a queer, award-winning poet who tours with Ani DiFranco,
releases a book of haunting, bold, nothing-but-the-truth ma'am poetry.

City of Insomnia (2008)
Victor D. Infante's noir-like exploration of unsentimental truth and poetic exorcism.

The Last Time as We Are (2009)
A new collection of poems from Taylor Mali, the author
of "What Teachers Make," the most forwarded poem in the world.

In Search of Midnight: the Mike Mcgee Handbook of Awesome (2009)
Slam's geek champion/class clown Mike McGee on his search for midnight
through hilarious prose, poetry, anecdotes, and how-to lists.

Over the Anvil We Stretch (2008)
2-time poetry slam champ Anis Mojgani's first collection: a Pushcart-Nominated
batch of backwood poetics, Southern myth, and rich imagery.

Animal Ballistics (2009)
Trading addiction and grief for empowerment and humor with her poetry,
Sarah Morgan does it best.

Rise of the Trust Fall (2010)
Award-winning feminist poet Mindy Nettifee
releases her second book of funny, daring, gorgeous, accessible poems.

No More Poems About the Moon (2008)
A pixilated, poetic and joyful view of a hyper-sexualized,
wholeheartedly confused, weird, and wild America with Michael Roberts.

Miles of Hallelujah (2010)
Slam poet/pop-culture enthusiast Rob "Ratpack Slim" Sturma
shows first collection of quirky, fantastic, romantic poetry.

Spiking the Sucker Punch (2009)
Nerd heartthrob, award-winning artist and performance poet,
Robbie Q. Telfer stabs your sensitive parts with his wit-dagger.

Racing Hummingbirds (2010)
Poet/performer Jeanann Verlee releases an award-winning book
of expertly crafted, startlingly honest, skin-kicking poems.

Live for a Living (2007)
Acclaimed performance poet Buddy Wakefield releases his second collection
about healing and charging into life face first.

WRITE BLOODY ANTHOLOGIES

The Elephant Engine High Dive Revival (2009)
Our largest tour anthology ever! Features unpublished work by
Buddy Wakefield, Derrick Brown, Anis Mojgani and Shira Erlichman!

The Good Things About America (2009)
American poets team up with illustrators to recognize the beauty and wonder in our
nation. Various authors. Edited by Kevin Staniec and Derrick Brown

Junkyard Ghost Revival (2008)
Tour anthology of poets, teaming up for a journey of the US in a small van.
Heart-charging, socially active verse.

The Last American Valentine:

Illustrated Poems To Seduce And Destroy (2008)
Acclaimed authors including Jack Hirschman, Beau Sia, Jeffrey McDaniel,
Michael McClure, Mindy Nettifee and more. 24 authors and 12 illustrators
team up for a collection of non-sappy love poetry. Edited by Derrick Brown

Learn Then Burn (2010)
Exciting classroom-ready anthology for introducing new writers
to the powerful world of poetry. Edited by Tim Stafford and Derrick Brown.

Learn Then Burn Teacher's Manual (2010)
Turn key classroom-safe guide Tim Stafford and Molly Meacham
to accompany *Learn Then Burn*: A modern poetry anthology for the classroom.

Knocking at the Door: Poems for Approaching the Other (2011)
An exciting compilation of diverse authors that explores the concept of the Other
from all angles. Innovative writing from emerging and established poets.

WWW.WRITEBLOODY.COM

Pull Your Books Up
By Their Bootstraps

WRITEBLOODY
QUALITY AMERICAN BOOKS

Write Bloody Publishing distributes and promotes great books of fiction, poetry and art every year. We are an independent press dedicated to quality literature and book design, with an office in Long Beach, CA.

Our employees are authors and artists so we call ourselves a family. Our design team comes from all over America: modern painters, photographers and rock album designers create book covers we're proud to be judged by.

We publish and promote 8-12 tour-savvy authors per year. We are grass-roots, D.I.Y., bootstrap believers. Pull up a good book and join the family. Support independent authors, artists and presses.

Visit us online:

WRITEBLOODY.COM

CPSIA information can be obtained at www.ICGtesting.com
Printed in the USA
268695BV00001B/9/P